★ IT'S MY STATE! ★
Oklahoma

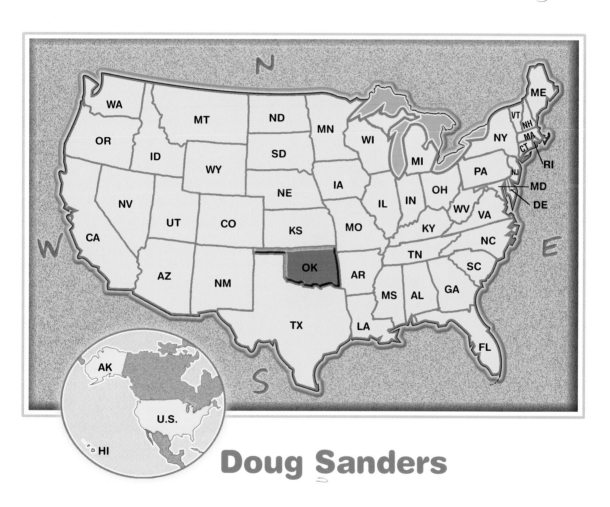

Doug Sanders

mc **Marshall Cavendish**
Benchmark
New York

Marshall Cavendish Benchmark
99 White Plains Road
Tarrytown, New York 10591-9001
www.marshallcavendish.us

Maps, text, and illustrations copyright © 2006 by Marshall Cavendish Corporation
Map on page 6 and illustrations by Christopher Santoro
Map on page 75 by Ian Worpole

Library of Congress Cataloging-in-Publication Data

Sanders, Doug.
Oklahoma / by Doug Sanders.
p. cm. — (It's my state!)
Summary: "Surveys the history, geography, economy, and people of
Oklahoma"—Provided by publisher.
Includes bibliographical references and index.
ISBN 0-7614-1906-3
1. Oklahoma—Juvenile literature. I. Title. II. Series.
F694.3.S26   2006   976.6—dc22   2005018056

Photo research by Candlepants Incorporated

Cover photograph: Mark Andersen / Rubberball / Picture Quest
Back cover illustration: The license plate shows Oklahoma's postal abbreviation followed by its year of statehood.

The photographs in this book are used by permission and through the courtesy of: *Corbis:* 22, 37; Tom Bean, 8; Danny Lehman, 10; William A. Bake, 13; Doug Hoke / The Oklahoman, 40; Bettmann, 41 (bottom), 48 (middle), 49 (bottom), 50; Lisa O'Connor / ZUMA, 49 (top); Hulton-Deutsch Collection, 49 (middle); Lindsay Hebberd, 52; Lowell Georgia, 68 (top). *Photo Researchers, Inc.:* Jeff Lepore, 4 (top); Alix, 4 (bottom); Dave Hosking, 5 (top); Ray Coleman, 5 (bottom); Adam Jones, 18 (top); David N. Davis, 18 (middle); Larry L. Miller, 19 (middle); David Schleser, 19 (bottom); Dante Fenolio, 21. *Animals Animals / Earth Scenes:* Darren Bennett, 4 (middle); Zigmund Leszczynski, 4 (middle); Lightwave Photography, Inc., 19 (top); Jim Steinberg, 16. *Bill Lindner Photography:* 18 (bottom). *The Image Works:* Topham, 15; Joe Sohm , 59. *PictureQuest:* Allen Russell, 64; John Hartman, 68 (middle); Paul Nevin, 69 (top); Hoa Qui, 69 (middle); Comstock Images, 69 (bottom). *SuperStock:* age footstock, 11; Lynn Radeka, 45; Bill Barley, 46; Steve Vidler, 62. *Index Stock:* Allen Russell, 12, 73; Jim Wark, 67; photolibrary.com pty. ltd, 68 (bottom); Ed Lallo, 70. *Oklahoma Archeological Survey, University of Oklahoma:* 24. *Art Resource, NY:* Smithsonian American Art Museum, Washington, DC, 25. *Courtesy, The Thomas Gilcrease Institute of American History and Art, Tulsa, Oklahoma:* 27. *Oklahoma Historical Society:* 31, 33, 38, 41 (top). *Oklahoma Tourism & Recreation Department:* 42, 44, 51, 53, 54, 55, 56, 71, 72. *Getty Images:* Time Life Pictures, 48 (top). *Envision Stock Photography:* Rita Maas, 65.

Book design by Anahid Hamparian

Printed in Malaysia

1   3   5   6   4   2

Contents

A Quick Look at Oklahoma

Nickname: The Sooner State
Population: 3,523,553 (2004 estimate)
Statehood: November 16, 1907

Tree: Redbud

In spring, the redbud's clusters of pinkish flowers often bloom before the heart-shaped leaves appear. The redbud became the official tree in 1937, prompting one poet to write, "And this is Oklahoma's tree of loveliness so rare, / A symbol of red earth and free, when blooming anywhere."

Bird: Scissor-Tailed Flycatcher

This bird almost missed its chance to be an official state symbol. In a vote held in 1929, the bobwhite was chosen but never officially adopted. But in May 1951, the flycatcher was officially adopted. It is known for its extremely long black-and-white tail as well as for the elaborate "sky dance" it performs to attract a mate.

Floral Emblem: Mistletoe

Though mistletoe is not really a flower, it became an official territory symbol in 1893, before Oklahoma was even a state. Mistletoe lives on trees that grow across the state. The dark green leaves and white berries of the plant are a common sight in Oklahoma in fall and winter.

Animal: Bison

At one point, bison filled North America, ranging from Alaska to northern Mexico. While the bison population once reached about 60 million, by the 1890s fewer than 1,000 still roamed the plains. As a result, concerned citizens began to protect this important American animal. Today bison can be seen in greater numbers on ranches, in parks and wildlife sanctuaries, and on the open plains.

Reptile: Collared Lizard

Oklahoma's collared lizards can frequently be seen sunning themselves in the Wichita Mountains. Early in the region's history, this silent reptile was nicknamed the "mountain boomer" by residents who were hearing loud noises. The settlers probably heard the loud calls of frogs and mistakenly thought the collared lizards were the source.

Butterfly: Black Swallowtail

As a caterpillar, this insect sports a vibrant pattern of white, black, and green stripes with rows of yellow dots. As a butterfly, the swallowtail is mostly black with bands or spots of yellow. Adults flit along the fields and roadsides of Oklahoma, drawing the nectar from plants such as red clover, milkweed, and thistle.

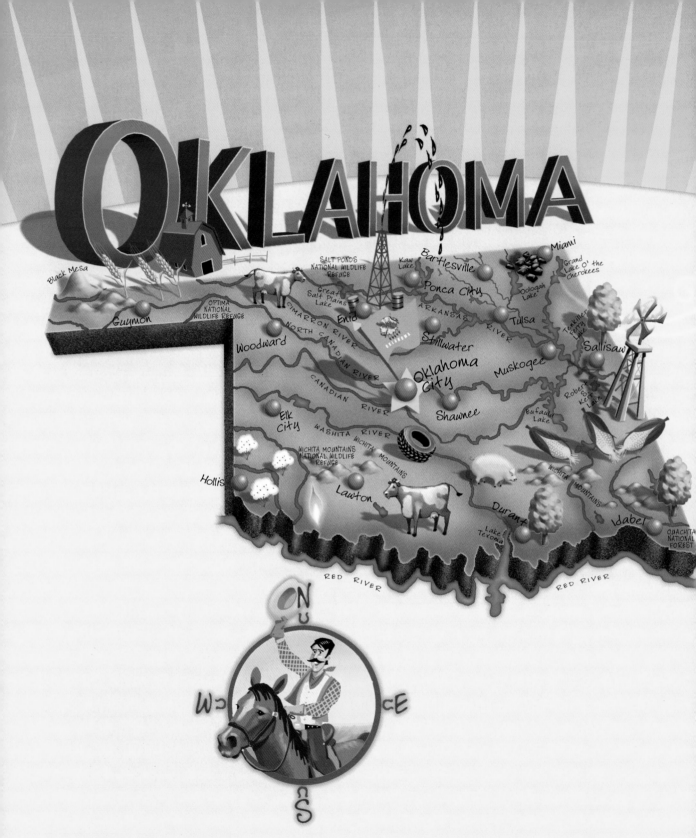

1 The Sooner State

Oklahoma's land is as varied as its people. Much of the state is made up of a massive rolling plain. It slopes gently downward as it unfolds from northwest to southeast. Those two compass points mark the two extremes of the state's geography and climate. The state's highest point is found at the tip of the Panhandle. The Panhandle is a strip of land 166 miles long and 34 miles wide. As its name suggests, it looks like a handle sticking out of the state's northwestern corner. It is there, near the border with New Mexico and Colorado, that Black Mesa is found. At 4,973 feet, Oklahoma's highest point offers great views of the surrounding area. The mesa—which is a small, isolated hill with steep sides—was created millions of years ago when lava oozed out of a nearby volcano. It hardened to form this high lookout Oklahomans treasure today.

Oklahoma's Borders
North: Colorado and Kansas
South: Texas
East: Arkansas and Missouri
West: Texas and New Mexico

Mesa means "table" in Spanish. These flat-topped hills with gently sloping sides mark the rolling landscape at Black Mesa Nature Preserve.

Oklahoma's lowest point in elevation is found at the opposite end of the state. Near Idabel, close to the border with Texas and Arkansas, the land dips to 289 feet. This region, extending north to the state's border with Missouri, is the most heavily forested part of Oklahoma. Almost one-quarter of the state is covered in trees, and many are found clustered in the east.

Of all the fifty states, Oklahoma ranks twentieth in the total area of its land and water. If you just count the land area, Oklahoma is nineteenth.

Eastern Oklahoma

Eastern Oklahoma is a region of flat, fertile plains and low hills. One of the most notable features is the Ozark Plateau. A plateau is a stretch of raised land with a nearly level surface. The

Ozark Plateau extends into the state from nearby Missouri and Arkansas. Residents often refer to this part of the state as Oklahoma's Green Country. Clear, swift-flowing rivers and streams help keep the area lush. The waters flow through steep-walled valleys, which break up the wide stretches of flat-topped uplands. The rivers helped create these valleys and the high bluffs that often line the banks. Over millions of years, the water's flow slowly carved these trenches into the land.

The southeastern part of Oklahoma is well forested and supports an active lumbering industry. The region is also home to the Ouachitas. They are one of the state's few mountain chains. The Ouachitas are made up of groups of tall sandstone ridges that stretch from west to east. The Ouachitas are among the most rugged land in the state. Natural springs bubble up and sparkling streams course in and out of the many valleys found tucked between the ridges.

Despite Oklahoma's highlands, the state is best known for its flatlands. Between the Ozark Plateau and the Ouachitas is the region known as the prairie plains. The term is used to describe land that is flat and mostly treeless. But it is better suited for agriculture than other parts of the Great Plains. (The Great Plains are a grassy region found in the central part of North America.) Crops thrive in this part of Oklahoma. East of Muskogee, the Arkansas River valley is an especially fertile part of the state. Much of the state's coal and major pockets of petroleum are also found there.

Central Oklahoma

Central Oklahoma also features a variety of landscapes. Starting on the northern edge of the state, near the border with Kansas,

Oklahoma's grassy plains yield a wealth of hay. These bales of hay will eventually help feed the herds of livestock that are so valuable to the state's economy.

the sandstone hills rise from 250 to 400 feet. Many of the hills are lined with blackjack and post oaks and other types of trees. The sandstone hills run almost the entire length of the state. This region includes Oklahoma's second-largest city, Tulsa.

In the south, the plains eventually give way to the rolling Red River region. This area of the state was important to Oklahoma's early petroleum industry. Today major oil fields are still found there, and in places crops thrive in the sandy soil.

The Red Bed Plains are found to the west of the sandstone hills. They form the largest land region in the state. Included in this region is the state's capital, Oklahoma City. Like the sandstone hills, this area stretches from the Kansas border to southern Oklahoma's boundary with Texas. A few forests are found in the eastern part of the plains. As the Red Beds gently slope upward to the west, they give way to grasslands. The land supports some farming and herding. The soil is made up of a combination of materials, mostly clay mixed in with harder layers of sandstone and gypsum. The region is crossed by several streams, which flow from the High Plains to the northwest.

A low-rising mountain chain adds to the variety of central Oklahoma as well. The Arbuckles cover about 1,000 square miles in the south-central part of the state. They are an ancient mountain system. Granite found in Johnston County is about 1.4 billion years old. That makes this part of the Arbuckles the oldest exposed rock between the southern Appalachians to the east and the Rocky Mountains to the west.

The Arbuckles were once tall peaks. But years of erosion have smoothed and flattened the range. They now rise from about 600 to 700 feet above the plains. They have lost some of their height but none of their value to Oklahomans. Nature lovers flock to the region. The Chickasaw National Recreation Area, Turner Falls, Price Falls, and the Arbuckle Wilderness Park are just some of the sites found in this part of the state. The Arbuckles also contain some of Oklahoma's richest collection of minerals. Iron ore, lead, zinc, limestone, and granite are just some of the mineral wealth these mountains contain.

Various natural springs flow out of the Arbuckle Mountains. Together they make up Honey Creek, which comes crashing down a 77-foot rock face in the form of Turner Falls, the state's largest waterfall.

Ending the tour of central Oklahoma is the thin strip along the border with Texas. Known as the Red River region, it extends all the way to the state's southeastern corner. There it meets up with the Ouachitas. This fertile area is known for its rolling prairie and forests. The sandy soil is among the state's richest. Vegetables are a common sight growing in the fields.

Western Oklahoma

Oklahoma's portion of the Great Plains is found to the west. This elevated region is made up mostly of thick grasslands. It is also home to wheat fields and the grazing lands that fatten many of the state's livestock. The area is also sometimes called the High Plains. The level grasslands rise gently from about 2,000 feet in the east to almost 5,000 feet at the western end of the Panhandle. This portion of Oklahoma is but a small part of the immense grasslands that reach from central Texas north into Canada. The smooth

Also called a prairie pothole, a sink or a playa lake serves as a much-needed oasis in the dry prairie. Livestock and various wildlife rely on the small pools as a valuable source of drinking water.

surface of the High Plains is broken only by large streams and circular features often called sinks or playa lakes. These small bodies of water are scattered across the plains and help support the area's wildlife.

But like the rest of the state, this part of Oklahoma has its own share of surprises. Sudden outcroppings of sandstone and gypsum, sharp ravines, and stark hills leave their mark on the northwest and the Panhandle. The southwest is also home to one of the state's most impressive mountain chains, the Wichitas. These granite peaks are about 525 million years old. They once towered 3,000 to 5,000 feet above the plains but, like the Arbuckles, millions of years of erosion have reduced their size.

Today the Wichitas range from 400 to 1,100 feet, though some peaks reach 2,400 feet. Mount Scott is perhaps the best-known peak in the range. Its summit, or highest point, can be reached on foot or by car or bus. It reveals some of the state's

most stunning scenery, including a great view of the region's many human-made lakes. These lakes were created by damming the many streams that flow out of the range. The area has become a valuable source of granite, lime-stone, and sand and gravel. Small-er amounts of gold, silver, copper, lead, zinc, aluminum, and iron ores are found in the Wichitas.

Cache Creek is one of the many waterways flowing out of the Wichitas.

The Gypsum Hills are another unique area in western Oklahoma. They lie west of the Red Bed Plains and eventually meet the High Plains in the northwestern portion of the state. These hills range in height from 150 to 200 feet. But it is not their size that is most impressive. Each of the hills is capped with a 15- to 20-foot layer of gypsum, a type of mineral. From a distance, they seem to sparkle in the sunlight. Because of that unique feature, they are sometimes called the Glass Hills.

This collection of buttes, mesas, and rolling hills appears to be a dry, almost desertlike region. But the area receives enough rainfall to be blanketed with a variety of wildflowers and prairie grasses such as little bluestem and hairy grama. Red cedars also dot the landscape.

Oklahoma has more human-made bodies of water than any other state. Most of the lakes are home to many different types of wildlife. Others are used for irrigation (to provide water for crops) or for recreational activities such as swimming, boating, and fishing.

Climate

Oklahoma is known for its warm, dry climate. Still the state sports a range of weather. The northwest tends to be cooler and a bit drier than areas in the southeast. Winter months can easily see the temperature dropping below 0 degrees Fahrenheit. North winds often descend on the Great Plains with their icy blasts.

In summer, opposite conditions are the rule. The sun beats down on the treeless grasslands, and few things stir during the height of the midday heat. Temperatures can often crawl well above 100 degrees. One thing that can break the relative summer calm is the threat of a tornado. On average, the state is visited by more than fifty of these dangerous and damaging weather systems

Oklahoma is home to Tornado Alley, a wide section of the state that gets hit by these swirling and dangerous storms.

each year. That ranks Oklahoma second in overall tornado frequency. Tornadoes damage property, claim lives, and are just one more reality the state's residents must try and adapt to.

Precipitation, the amount of moisture the state receives, can vary greatly throughout the state. The southeast averages about 50 inches of precipitation per year. That is a lot of moisture when compared to the 15 average inches the Panhandle receives. As for snow, few people think Oklahomans ever see any. But residents in the southeast can receive light storms, dropping an average of 2 inches on the region. People living in the Panhandle, though, often have to shovel their way through up to 25 inches per year.

Wild Life

Oklahoma's terrain is diverse. This great variety means the state is home to a wide range of plants and animals. Forests cover between 20 and 25 percent of the state. Oak, hickory, elm, pine, and ash are some of the trees that make up the woodlands of the east and southeast. White-tailed deer, raccoon, foxes, squirrels, and opossums make their homes in and among the trees.

Being a prairie state, Oklahoma is also known for its wild grasses. These grasses help to feed the state's livestock and have colorful names such as bluestem, grama, wire grass, and sand grass. But grasses are not the only plants on the prairie. Sagebrush, mesquite, goldenrod, sunflowers, and black-eyed Susans are just a few of the other hearty plants that thrive on the plains. Black-tailed jackrabbits, pocket gophers, and kit foxes move through the thick grass.

Oklahoma's tallgrass prairie features a rich blend of native grasses, wildflowers, and a small group of trees, called a gallery forest, clustered near a rare water source.

With so many human-made reservoirs and lakes, the state is a fisherman's paradise. Oklahoma is bass country, but the state's fishermen head out in search of anything that bites. Sunfish, crappies, catfish, and carp gather near the shore or swim along the bottoms of the state's waterways.

The skies of Oklahoma are the site of an equally impressive collection of animals. Often large flocks blot the sky, or a single bird can be seen soaring—the only thing moving above the empty plains. Meadowlarks perch on fenceposts, tilt back their heads, and fill the air with song. Blue jays, cardinals, doves, crows, and mockingbirds gather as well. They are just some of the many bird species found in the Sooner State.

The Gypsum Hills are another great place to see the range of plants and animals the state has to offer. Bobcats and coyotes pad about the underbrush in search of a meal. Black-tailed prairie dogs keep a constant watch near their underground dens. They scurry down their holes at the first sign of danger. Armadillos, deer, and roadrunners are common sights as well. Collared lizards, western rattlesnakes, and tarantulas can be found in the shade, hiding from the hot rays of the midday sun.

Under many of the bridges and outcroppings found in the Gypsum Hills, colonies of cliff swallows build their hanging nests out of mud. The fruit of the area's many red cedars draw winged visitors from far away. During the winter, flocks of mountain bluebirds descend on the region, hundreds of miles from where they usually make their homes. They feed in the cedars, which also draw a number of birds that have headed south for the winter. Robins, cedar waxwings, and Townsend's solitaires can also be seen flitting among the trees.

Plants & Animals

Wild Turkey

The wild turkey is Oklahoma's official state game bird. Two species call the state home. The Rio Grande turkey is found in large numbers across the state, and the eastern wild turkey is located mostly in the state's southeastern and northeastern parts. Once threatened, today the state's gobbler population is on the rise.

Armadillo

The bony, scaly shell of the nine-banded armadillo protects it from predators. Armadillos are good diggers as well as good swimmers. They eat insects, grubs, and occasionally berries and birds' eggs. Female nine-banded armadillos are unique because when they reproduce, they give birth to four identical babies.

White Bass

Across the state, on lakes and reservoirs, patient fishermen wait to hook these bass, which are also called sand bass. The state "Sandies" as they are often called, travel in large schools, or groups. They eat other fish—mostly shad—and insects as well. The white bass is Oklahoma's state fish.

Prairie Rattlesnake

If you are hiking in the wilds of Oklahoma, keep your eyes peeled for these serpents coiled beneath rocks. While they are rarely deadly to humans, the snakes' venom can be twice as strong as other rattlesnakes' in the region. The prairie rattlesnake lives mainly in the grasslands, but in winter it moves to dens in outcroppings and rocky ledges. They feed on small rodents, birds that nest on the ground, and sometimes other snakes.

Red Bat

These nighttime flyers are unique in the bat world. They are the only species of bat in North America in which the female and male are different colors. The females tend to be yellow-brown, while the males can be a bright shade of orange. Red bats roost in trees, and can eat more than 1,000 insects per hour.

Indian Blanket

The Indian blanket is Oklahoma's state wildflower. It usually blooms from June to August and reaches from 1 to 3 feet in height. The flower is red in the center with yellow on the tips. A fitting symbol of the Sooner State, the Indian blanket thrives in both extreme heat and drought conditions, much like the people who call Oklahoma home.

Endangered

Oklahomans love their land and work hard to protect the plants and animals that live there. They try and make sure the state's many species have healthy populations. That takes cooperation. Almost 95 percent of the state's land is privately owned. When there are problems, owners must agree to let wildlife officials step in and offer a solution. Too often, officials and groups take action when a species is already threatened or when the population of that species has become dangerously low. But concerned Oklahomans use a different approach. They want to prevent species from being harmed or threatened in the first place. They help ailing plant and animal communities recover and increase their numbers in the state before it is too late.

A government program, Partners for Fish and Wildlife Program, was started in Oklahoma in 1990. It works to restore land and improve animal populations on privately owned lands across the state. Over the past decade and a half, the program has met with great success. Part of that success comes from working with a variety of groups and concerned citizens in the state. Together they have improved the quality of life for several species.

At first, the program targeted wetlands. Later, wildlife officials focused on improving the areas where threatened and endangered plants and animals live. A total of 446 projects are currently under way in practically every Oklahoma county. So far the Fish and Wildlife Program has restored more than 63,000 acres of land where Oklahoma's wildlife make their home. That includes more than 13,000 acres of prairie wetlands. These are valuable areas upon which migrating birds and a range of local species depend.

Even creatures living in out-of-the-way places need special protection. An endangered species, the Ozark cavefish is blind and lives underground, usually in the pools found in caverns. With its lack of eyes and whitish color, the creature is also referred to as the "ghost fish."

But conservation workers and concerned citizens know that it takes more than just projects. They believe that education is the key to ensuring the future of Oklahoma's wildlife. So they have set up almost seventy outdoor environmental classrooms. In these settings, students can learn more about the world around them and what they can do to make a difference. Program officials estimate more than 2 million students will use these special outdoor learning centers over the course of the next twenty years. Officials hope that after these children attend the programs, they will go back to their communities with a better understanding of how valuable their state's land and animals really are.

2 From the Beginning

Humans have been living in Oklahoma for more than 11,000 years. At a site near Anadarko, archaeologists—scientists who study the past—found several spear points and the bones of a mammoth (a large mammal that is now extinct). They have connected these artifacts with a group of people known as the Clovis culture. This ancient group most likely wandered into the region following the roaming herds of animals. The plains proved to be an ideal place to search for food. Many prehistoric creatures came to the grasslands to graze and mate. Giant mammoths, musk ox, ground sloths, elk, reindeer, bears, and an early version of the horse all made the plains their home.

Eventually these early people of the Clovis culture shifted their focus to one main food source—the bison. Small groups of people would follow the wandering herds for part or most of the year. They would then return to camps where they stayed for a brief time in temporary shelters before they once again moved on.

Five-year-old Jewel and six-year-old Harold Walker pause from their chores on their farm in Comanche County in 1916. On an average day, they could pick up to 25 pounds of cotton.

23

Oklahoma's Mound Builders left their permanent mark on the state in places such as Spiro Mounds.

They also gathered plants, eating whatever they could find.

Then about 2,500 years ago, another shift occurred. People settled into a more stable lifestyle. Farming, mostly of corn and beans, became an important source of food.

From 500 to 1300 CE, a group known as the Mound Builders lived in what would become LaFlore County, just west of the Arkansas-Oklahoma border. They built huge earthen mounds to honor their dead. Artifacts found in these burial mounds show that the Mound Builders made artwork and many useful objects by hand. They also had a complex economy that involved a large trading network. It stretched from the Great Lakes to the Pacific coast. Over the centuries, communities became larger and more established. Distinct native groups emerged.

The Native Past

From the ancient past to the present, Oklahoma has been a cross-roads of Native American life. The Caddo were an early nation, centered in the southeast. The Cheyenne and the Arapaho were latecomers to the plains. They abandoned their settled lives centered on farm communities and took to hunting bison.

Grass houses, like the one in this painting by George Catlin, were the ideal home for the Wichita. The structures—light, cool, and strong—were suited to the state's climate.

They moved from place to place in search of food. In some cases, they also raided other villages and towns for food. The Comanche and Plains Apache roamed the west, also following the bison herds. The Quapaw settled in the northeast as farmers and hunter-gatherers.

The Wichita adopted a similar lifestyle. They built grass houses often along rivers and streams in the southern and eastern parts of the area. The later arrivals in the northeast, the Osage, mostly farmed. But their hunting parties made

> Oklahoma's name comes from combining two Choctaw words—*okla* meaning "people" and *humma* or *homma* meaning "red." So the state's name means "red people."

annual bison hunts on the plains to the west. They also conducted raids on Wichita villages. The Kiowa and Pawnee were other major native nations, adding to the great variety of tribes living on the Oklahoma plains.

Europeans Arrive

The first European to enter Oklahoma was most likely Francisco Vásquez de Coronado. He crossed the region in 1541, leading an expedition that started in present-day New Mexico. Hernando de Soto, another Spanish explorer, may have passed through eastern Oklahoma as well. They were both in search of gold and, finding none, soon moved on.

In 1601 Juan de Oñate also traveled through the western portion of the state in search of gold. His group reached present-day Wichita, Kansas, then turned around and headed back to the Southwest. Onate was followed by additional Spanish explorers and French traders from Louisiana looking for new markets for their goods. Rene-Robert Cavelier, Sieur de La Salle, had first claimed the area for France on his trek down the Mississippi River valley. But these newcomers found little to make them stay in the region.

The first European trading post was most likely established at Salina in the opening years of the 1800s. Then, with the Louisiana Purchase of 1803, the area came under United States control. A few other important early settlements sprang up, including Miller Court House, located in McCurtain County, and Three Forks. But beyond the occasional trader, explorer, or curious traveler, the region stayed in the hands of the Native Americans. Because of the area's remote location and the isolation of the plains, most Natives did not come into contact with outsiders until the 1800s. The Wichita and other nations first introduced items they had received in trade from the Europeans. Beads, cloth, cookware, and weapons were just some of the items that changed Native life. These items were the first traces of the many white settlers who would eventually come from the East.

After the War of 1812, problems began brewing in the East that would affect the region for years to come. The United States government began its campaign to remove and relocate certain Natives from the southeastern states. Known as the Five Civilized Tribes, the Cherokee, Choctaw, Chickasaw, Creek, and Seminole

home for hundreds of years. Now they were forced to leave their homeland behind and enter the strange new landscape of the Great Plains. To prepare for the large number of newcomers, officials built forts, including Forts Towson and Gibson. The forts also allowed the United States government to keep a watchful eye on the borders.

Few of the Natives came of their own free will. At first, thousands of Cherokee and other Native peoples were moved to the unclaimed "no-man's-land" of the southern plains. One-third of the Cherokee Nation died while making this journey, now known as the Trail of Tears. The survivors

The Trail of Tears ended as a death march—a journey that claimed one-third of the Cherokee forced to the west.

eventually settled on the hills and plains of eastern Oklahoma. There they set about the hard work of rebuilding their communities and their lives. But their arrival was just the first of many. The forced migration continued from 1830 to 1842.

All of Oklahoma, except for the Panhandle, was set aside for the Native Americans. Over time, the relocated groups settled into their new homeland. They each formed their own new nations. They built homes and schools and established courts and legislatures, or groups that set up tribal laws. The Cherokee and Choctaw grew cotton, while the Creek and Chickasaw mostly herded livestock.

Making a Cherokee Bear Claw Necklace

All of the Native Americans who moved into Oklahoma Indian Territory were proud of the traditional crafts they brought from their ancestral lands. Jewelry was one of the treasured art forms. By following these instructions you can make an imitation of a bear claw necklace worn by members of the Cherokee nation.

What You Need
Several sheets of newspaper
Self-hardening clay—about a 1 lb.
   package (found at craft stores)
Ruler
Butter knife
Large nail or knitting needle
Acrylic paints—in any color
Paint brushes
2 feet of twine (or shoelaces or rawhide lacing)

Spread the newspaper on your work surface because the clay can get messy. Take the clay out of the package and knead it for a few minutes to soften it. Pull off a small piece of clay and roll it into a bear claw shape, about 1-1/2 inches long and no more than 1/4 inch thick. You can use the knife to help you shape the clay, but be careful since the knife can be sharp. (You can ask an adult for help cutting and shaping the clay.) Make four more claws, all about the same size. For all five claws, have an adult help you use the knitting needle or nail to make a hole through the thickest part of each claw. Set aside the claws while you make the clay beads.

Break off four small pieces of clay. With your fingers, roll them out to make long bone beads about 1/2 inch thick and 3/4 inch long. Carefully push the nail or knitting needle through each.

Break off ten small pieces of clay and roll them into small round beads. Carefully push the nail or knitting needle through each of these beads.

Put all the claws and beads in a flat, dry place and let these clay pieces harden. This should take about one to two days.

Once the clay pieces are dry, get ready to paint them. Spread more newspaper on your work surface. Using the acrylic paints, paint the bear claws a dark brown, and the long bone beads white. You can use any other colors for the small round beads.

While the paint is drying, take the twine or lacing and cut a piece long enough to drape around your neck like a necklace. When the paint is dry, string the beads onto the twine or lacing. Alternate claws, bone beads, and round beads in whatever pattern you like. Tie the ends of the twine together—use a double-knot to make sure it stays tied. You can wear your necklace or show it to your friends and family.

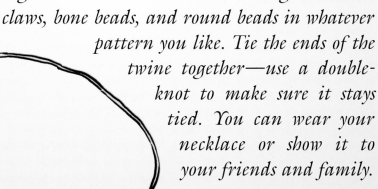

The Civil War and Beyond

From 1861 to 1865, the North and South were engaged in the Civil War. During this war, no major battles were fought in Oklahoma. The region was located too far west to be directly involved in the battles. But several minor skirmishes played out on Oklahoma soil. The region remained divided in its loyalties. Having come from the South, many of the members of the relocated Native American nations owned slaves. When it came time to choose sides, a majority of the Indians supported the South— also called the Confederacy. At first, the Cherokee were reluctant to favor either the Union (the North) or the Confederacy. But representatives from Texas and Arkansas (both states were part of the Confederacy) met with them, urging them to support the South. Eventually the Cherokee Nation agreed and sided with the Confederacy.

One famed Cherokee, Stand Watie, became a brigadier general in the Confederate Army.

Though both sides lost many lives and battles, the Union won the Civil War. At the end of the war, Oklahoma's Native American nations realized they had chosen unwisely. As punishment for siding with the Confederacy, the western part of the Indian Territory (land granted to the Five Civilized Tribes) was taken away. It was divided among other Native American nations forced from their lands in the East, as well as among certain Plains groups that government officials had been hoping to control. New Native faces now staked their claim to the plains. The Peoria, Ottawa, Wyandot, and Miami moved west and began farming the Oklahoma countryside. Cheyenne, Kiowa, Comanche, and Arapaho, used to the freedom of the wide-open spaces of the plains, had more difficulty adjusting to the often cramped living conditions on the reservations.

With the Kiowa, Comanche, Cheyenne, and Arapaho, the United States signed the Little Arkansas Treaties. The Native American nations agreed to remain peaceful and to reduce the size of their hunting ranges. In exchange, the United States government vowed to protect and support the Native nations. The Native Americans were promised they would own and govern their new homelands. But the United States Senate refused to approve the treaties. Officials had little concern for protecting Native rights. In addition, the flow of mostly white settlers onto the southern plains increased. Soon the newcomers pushed up against the borders of Native American land. The unclaimed miles of free land surrounding Indian Territory were soon taken. Non-Native people seeking a new and better life along the American frontier flooded into the region. To make matters worse, hunters—mostly from the East—killed tens of thousands of bison, taking an important source of food away from the Native Americans.

Buffalo hunters set up camp along the plains in the 1870s. Not only was the animal driven to the brink of extinction, but the Native Americans who relied on the bison for food, clothing, and shelter were dealt a severe blow to their way of life.

The Little Arkansas was just one of many treaties and many broken promises. But the pattern was set. Oklahoma's native residents soon realized the United States government cared little of what happened to them. A series of attacks on settlers began in the summer of 1867. The United States Army stepped in and quickly ended the violence. More treaties resulted in the creation of more reservation lands. The Kiowa and Comanche were given 3 million acres, while the Cheyenne and Arapaho were granted 5 million. The great era of the Plains Indian was slowly coming to an end.

The Changing Plains

With the arrival of so many new faces, the region's economy began to grow and expand. The area became a crossroads for the thousands of cattle being moved from the ranches of Texas to the railroad in Kansas. Ranchers drove their herds across the state, pausing to fatten the valuable animals on the green ranges of Oklahoma. Some cattlemen paid the Native Americans for the right to have their herds graze on the Native-held lands. Most did not.

Soon, well-traveled cattle trails lined the region. The Chisholm Trail became the best known, but the Western, East Shawnee, and West Shawnee trails soon became heavily used as well. Between 1866 and 1885, more than 6 million head of Texas longhorn cattle crossed Native American lands. Slowly ranchers became more and more convinced of the value of owning what was once considered the bleak and useless Oklahoma land. When the railroad came to Oklahoma in the early 1870s, the region became even more valuable in the eyes of herders and settlers alike.

Boomers

As Oklahoma's Native Americans were moved onto reservations, many settlers grew anxious to claim the lands for themselves. Called boomers, they were led by William L. Couch, C. C. Carpenter, and David L. Payne. They put pressure on the government to open the Oklahoma lands to settlement.

Eventually the government yielded. From the Creek and the Seminole, it bought more than 3 million acres. This parcel was added to the lands taken from other Indian nations. Almost two-thirds of the area, a large part of central Oklahoma, was then declared open for settlement in 1889. On April 22, anxious land-grabbers lined up along the territorial border, awaiting the signal to head into the region. At noon the land was officially opened. The signal brought a mad dash as settlers raced into the unclaimed miles. They were in search of a prime stretch of Oklahoma countryside to call their own. Those who had snuck

When the territory was opened for settlement in 1889, the land grab—the race to claim the valuable acres—was on.

into the territory illegally, before the official signal, were known as Sooners. The description has remained a nickname for Oklahoma's residents ever since.

On the morning of April 22, 1889, Oklahoma City was a stretch of barren prairie. By nightfall, more than 10,000 people had descended on the region and called the area home.

Territory and Statehood

Originally set aside as Indian Territory in 1834, on May 2, 1890, the region was then divided into two parts. One was still called Indian Territory, while the other was named the Oklahoma Territory. Indian Territory included the remaining lands of the Five Civilized Tribes plus other limited holdings settled by other tribes. It was also at this time that the territory acquired the Panhandle, a strip of land that had once belonged to Texas. George W. Steele was named the first territorial governor.

September 16, 1893, saw the largest land rush in the territory's history. That was the day the Cherokee Outlet, in the north-central part of the region, as well as the Tonkana and Pawnee Reservations, were first opened to white settlers. More than 50,000 people descended on the region claiming the land that made up the 6-1/2-million-acre parcel. But many of the newcomers were not prepared for the hard life they faced on the open plains. All they saw was free land and not the challenges and responsibilities that came with it. For every farm that succeeded, many others failed.

Many homesteaders, as these settlers were also called, abandoned the plots of land they had once raced across the Oklahoma countryside to claim. Wealthy land owners, often called land barons, bought up these empty plots. Later, those settlers who arrived in the territory in the early 1900s found there was only land to rent, not own. Sharecropping became the normal course in some places. By 1900, 40 percent of Oklahoma's farmers were tenant farmers, the highest number in the nation. Tenant farmers rented the land from the owner and then paid the landowner a portion of their crops in exchange.

In 1893 a special committee called the Dawes Commission was set up to divide some of the remaining Native American lands into smaller pieces. These parcels of land were to go to individuals or native families. Officials saw the program as a way of ending what little control some Indian nations still had over their large tracts of land. Agents helped the Natives set up towns and prepare to become American citizens. Slowly, Indian Territory became a mixture of white settlers and Native people who owned their own private plot of land. The population grew. By 1905, Indian Territory was ready for statehood. So the Five Civilized Tribes called a constitutional convention at Muskogee. White settlers were invited to take part as well. They outnumbered the Native Americans five to one. At the end of the convention, all had agreed to create the state of Sequoyah. The action was then approved by the voters in Indian Territory.

But Congress refused to recognize their petition to become a state. The United States government had other plans for the area. Officials wanted to create one state out of Oklahoma and Indian territories. So delegates from each territory met in Guthrie in 1906. They agreed to combine the two territories, and on November 16, 1907, Oklahoma officially became a state. At the time, its population totaled more than 1.4 million. Guthrie was named the first state capital. But in 1910, it was moved to Oklahoma City.

In this first decade of the 1900s, the state's economy boomed.

The oil industry had become well established by this time. The first drilling, a small well, occurred near Chelsea in 1889. The first major operation was later begun in Bartlesville in 1897. When the Red Fork-Tulsa oil field opened in 1901, Tulsa became the oil capital of the new state.

Cattle ranching, though on the decline, was also still a major source of the state's income. At the same time, crops such as corn, wheat, and cotton added as well to Oklahoma's wealth. But farming was still a hard life for many of Oklahoma's residents. Crop prices fell, and the state's farmers found that they needed more and more land to squeeze a profit from their farms.

Dust Bowl Days

With the arrival of World War I, the nation had an increased demand for crops and food products, which Oklahoma's farmers helped to supply. But after this short period of prosperity, the state's fortunes took a grave turn. Farm prices dropped again. The Ku Klux Klan (KKK), a secret organization that supported violence against African Americans and other minorities, gained in popularity across the state. Their influence spread to city and county governments, in which they held certain key seats of power. In 1921, in one of Tulsa's darkest moments, angry white mobs threatened to kill an African-American man falsely accused of hurting a white woman. When residents of the African-American neighborhood of Greenwood resisted, violence erupted. Angry Tulsans burned most of the neighborhood. As many as 300 African-American residents were killed.

Away from the cities, another threat was gaining force. Drought spread across the plains. At the same time, the need for

Not every Okie family headed west. With only the belongings they could carry, this migrant family takes to the road in this photograph from 1938. The hopeful group walked from Idabel to Krebs in search of work and a new and better life.

wheat and other crops declined. The state's fields were overplanted and the soil had been overworked and drained of its nutrients. Farm prices fell and banks closed, taking people's life savings with them. Extremely hot summers and the lack of rain only made matters worse. Crops withered and died in the fields.

Overgrazing from the state's many cattle had also removed much of the grass from the topsoil. High winds whipped up, carrying huge clouds of soil and dirt with it. At times, the clouds were so large and so thick, residents said it appeared as if it had suddenly become night-time in the middle of the day. Oklahoma found itself located in the heart of what was known as the Dust Bowl.

Many of the state's farmers, miners, and oil workers felt they had no other choice but to leave. Okies, as they were called, moved west in the hope of leaving the hard times behind them. As a result, the state lost more than 300,000 residents.

But times were tough everywhere. The nation was in the grips of the Great Depression, which had started in 1929. It was a time in which millions of Americans had no jobs and families struggled to get by.

Eventually the drought ended. People had learned a harsh lesson from the Dust Bowl years and began to use the land more wisely. With the onset of World War II, as well as with aid from the federal government, the state's economy slowly improved. The war meant that once again the state's two main products—crops and oil—were in greater demand. Military bases, built outside of Enid and Oklahoma City, also created much-needed jobs.

As the focus of the state's economy shifted, once-small communities, such as Elk City, shown in the 1950s, became thriving centers of the gas and oil industries.

To the Present Day

The second half of the twentieth century brought even more changes to the state. Leaders and residents worked hard to improve life in the state and to build and strengthen the economy. One major focus was on irrigation and developing the state's farmlands. Several major projects, such as the reservoir created by the Kerr Dam along the Arkansas River, were begun. They not only improved growing conditions but created state recreation areas as well. But at the same time, starting in the 1950s, the state's economy began slowly shifting its focus.

Factories and manufacturing would eventually replace agriculture as the state's top earner. Fewer farms marked the miles of grasslands, as cities and towns grew.

Strong governors continued to guide the state, reforming education, prisons, and the ways the state handled its finances. New industries and new construction projects boosted the state's economy in the 1960s. Electronics plants were built in Oklahoma City. The state capital also became the home of a major center for the Federal Aviation Administration (FAA). This important facility trained airport workers and conducted research into airplane safety. Farther east, Tulsa became the site of factories in which parts for spaceships were built.

In the 1970s, the state continued to achieve major successes. New businesses opened as the state began highlighting its major selling points—its abundance of space, fuel, water, and electric power. In 1971, the Oklahoma portion of the Arkansas River Navigation System opened. It gave the cities of Muskogee and Tulsa—at its port in Catoosa on the Verdigris River—direct access to the coastal centers. Like the rest of the nation, Oklahoma was slowly becoming more and more connected to the growing global economy.

A dramatic rise in oil prices brought another unexpected boost to the state's economy. But in the 1980s, when prices fell once again, the state's economy experienced a dip similar to the one in the 1930s. Oil wells across the state were shut down. The state recovered slowy.

The 1990s were marked by the further growth of the economy, as the state looked for new ways of earning its income. New businesses were lured to the state, requiring new types of worker, trained in an ever wider variety of skills.

Tourism, service, and technology became three swiftly expanding areas in Oklahoma's economy.

On April 19, 1995, another dark chapter was added to the state's history. A terrorist bomb ripped through a government building on an otherwise quiet morning in Oklahoma City. In what became the second-worst terrorist act in American history, 168 Oklahomans lost their lives. A new memorial, at the site where the bombed building once stood, makes sure that people will never forget those who lost their lives in this tragedy. People from across the country and around the world continue to visit the city. Many come to pay tribute to the spirit and bravery of a people who know how to work together and make the best out of tough times.

Empty chairs—covered in flowers and wreaths—stand for the 168 people who died when a bomb ripped through a government building in Oklahoma Cityon April 19, 1995.

Important Dates

1500s   Several Native American nations, including the Arapaho, Caddo, Kiowa, Osage, Pawnee, and Wichita, reside in the state.

1541   Francisco Vásquez de Coronado becomes the first European to enter Oklahoma, when he and his party cross the Panhandle in search of gold.

1682   Oklahoma is claimed for the French crown by La Salle.

1762   France gives its New World holdings, including Oklahoma, to Spain.

1800   Oklahoma once again is returned to French control.

1803   Oklahoma, included in the Louisiana Purchase, becomes part of the United States.

1819   All of the state, except for the Panhandle, becomes part of the newly formed Territory of Arkansas.

1824   Forts Gibson and Towson are built in the territory.

1830s–1842 The Five Civilized Tribes are relocated to Oklahoma.

1872   The first railway line is laid across the region.

1889   Oklahoma is opened to settlement.

1890   The Oklahoma Territory is created.

1907   Oklahoma becomes the forty-sixth state.

1921   Racial violence in Tulsa claims about 300 African-American lives.

1928   The Oklahoma City oil field is opened.

1930s   Severe drought earns parts of the state the nickname the Dust Bowl. Thousands leave the state in search of opportunity elsewhere.

1970   The Arkansas River Navigation System is finished, allowing barges to travel from the Gulf of Mexico to Tulsa.

1990   The state becomes the first to put limits on the number of terms its state legislators can serve.

1995   A terrorist's bomb destroys the Alfred E. Murrah Federal Building in Oklahoma City, killing 168 people.

2007   Oklahoma celebrates 100 years of statehood.

Stand Watie

Oil wells

3 The People

When Oklahoma became the forty-sixth state in 1907, its residents were already a blend of many cultures and traditions. They were made up of southern cotton farmers, Midwestern wheat farmers, and western cattlemen. Smaller numbers of Native Americans, African Americans, and European immigrants also added to the mix. The geography of the state helped to draw such a wide variety of people. Oklahoma does not belong to a single part of the country. Instead it is spread over several regions. South, West, and Midwest all come together to give the state its unique flavor and appeal. While some came to farm the land, others were drawn by the rise of the petroleum industry.

When the coal fields near McAlester were opened in the late 1800s, European immigrants flooded into the region. Newcomers from Wales, Ireland, Poland, Russia, Italy, France, and Lithuania made the area one of the most diverse in the territory.

Other groups created their own towns on the plains. German Mennonites from Russia brought sacks of Crimean hard wheat to their new homes. They started farming communities

A possible future bull rider takes in the action at the Rodeo of Champions in Elk City.

Many ethnic groups have added to the diversity the state enjoys today. Dressed in colorful traditional costumes, these girls are taking part in a Czech festival that kicks off each year in Yukon.

named Corn, Colony, and Bessie in western Oklahoma. Czech immigrants, mostly arriving from other parts of the Midwest, built the towns of Prague, Yukon, and Mishak. Slaves freed by the Native Americans, as well as new arrivals from the South, built a chain of black towns across the plains. Boley, Red Bird, Rentiesville, and Langston are just a few of the communities that still exist to this day.

In recent years, new groups have arrived. They are adding to the changing face of Oklahoma. But no matter how diverse the newcomers may be, many people are drawn to the state for similar reasons. Community pride, good schools, and a slower pace help make the Sooner State a

A quiet afternoon in downtown Guthrie. The state's residents are proud of their small towns that offer an alternative to big city life—a slower pace, little or no crime, and a strong sense of community.

great place to live. Like the rest of the country, the state's suburbs are growing. "People are leaving the hustle and bustle of the big town," said Jeff Wallace, director of the Oklahoma State Data Center. More and more Oklahomans want to settle down in places that are safe and have a strong sense of community.

A Blend of Cultures

Hispanics are one group that has seen great growth in the state. This is part of a nationwide trend. But while the nation's Hispanic population grew by 58 percent during the 1990s, in Oklahoma that figure equaled 108 percent. That means the

Through the years, Tulsa has emerged as a bustling center of international business.

size of the state's Hispanic community has more than doubled in a brief period of time.

The state's cities have seen most of the growth, as urban jobs have drawn people from across the country and around the world. Hispanics made up more than half of the population increase in Oklahoma City, the state's largest urban center. Many city residents now consider their hometown a "big city" as its population has reached 500,000 for the first time. Tulsa has expanded its numbers as well, where one-third of the city's new residents are Hispanic.

"The biggest increase was, of course, from Hispanic

growth," said Jeff Wallace. "But we also had a substantial increase in [Asian residents]." Officials cite a few reasons for the increase. While the cities will always draw newcomers to the state, the growth of farming in the northwestern part of the state has drawn Asian as well as Hispanic immigrants. Hog farming and processing have increased in that portion of Oklahoma creating hundreds of new jobs along with it.

Another reason for the increased Asian presence is a second wave of immigrants from Vietnam. After the Vietnam War ended in the early 1970s, many Vietnamese families came to the United States. But moving to a new country can be expensive, and often relatives were left behind. Today Oklahoma is seeing a steady stream of Vietnamese immigrants entering the region. Across the state, families are being reunited with relatives they have not seen, in some cases, for almost thirty years. Other Asians and Asian Americans are also making Oklahoma their home. They are drawn by the jobs, schools, and communities.

African Americans

African Americans, whose numbers in Oklahoma surpassed 279,000 in the early 2000s, remain the state's largest minority. They have had a rich and long history in the state, first arriving with the Cherokee along the Trail of Tears. Most of the first black Oklahomans were slaves owned by the members of the Five Civilized Tribes. When the Native Americans were forced west, their slaves came with them. In parts of Oklahoma, some Native Americans were able to re-create life much as they had known back in the South. One Choctaw plantation totaled more than 5,000 acres and contained 500 slaves.

Famous Oklahomans

Ralph Ellison: Writer

Born in Oklahoma City, Ellison studied briefly at Alabama's Tuskegee Institute before moving to New York City to study sculpture. But soon writing became his passion. His 1952 novel, Invisible Man, *won the National Book Award and became an instant classic. It tells the story of an African-American man who is losing his identity in a racist world. It is considered by many to be one of the best American novels of the century.*

Shannon Lucid: Astronaut

Lucid grew up in Bethany. After receiving a Ph.D. from the University of Oklahoma, she became one of the first six women chosen by NASA to be an astronaut. Currently she holds the American record for total time spent in space. During her 1996 mission aboard the Mir space station, she traveled more than 75 million miles. She conducted a variety of experiments during the mission, including growing wheat while in orbit. "It reminded me of Oklahoma," she said.

Robert S. Kerr: Politician and Oilman

Born in 1896 in a log cabin near Ada, Kerr became Oklahoma's governor in 1943, becoming the first Oklahoma-born resident to hold that position. He then went on to serve for fifteen years in the U.S. Senate, where he represented the interests of the oil and gas industry. Kerr is also responsible for helping to plan dams and waterways linking the Arkansas River to ocean ports.

Reba McEntire: Singer and Actress

This country singer started performing at the age of five. She first turned heads as a singer when she sang the national anthem at a rodeo in Oklahoma City. Since then, McEntire has sold millions of albums and has received two Grammy Awards. In recent years, the McAlister-born redhead has acted in movies and miniseries and stars in her own television show.

Maria Tallchief: Ballerina

Born in Fairfax of Scottish-Irish and Native American parents, Tallchief eventually went on to study dance in California. When choreographer George Balanchine founded the New York City Ballet in 1948, he chose Tallchief as its prima ballerina. Together they set the tone for American dance for two decades. With the company, she performed around the world, appearing as a guest star with dance companies in Paris and Copenhagen. She retired from the world of dance in 1966, and in 1996, she was chosen for a Kennedy Center Honor.

Mickey Mantle: Baseball Player

Born in Spavinaw in 1931, this talented switch-hitting power hitter played high school sports before getting signed by the New York Yankees where he played for eighteen years. During his time with the Yankees, he led the league in home runs four times, received the Triple Crown (for batting average, home runs, and RBIs) and three MVP awards, and helped lead his team to the World Series title seven times. In 1974, Mantle was elected to the Baseball Hall of Fame.

Later, African Americans came to the region as farmers, cowboys, homesteaders, and businesspeople. During the Civil War, runaway slaves and people of mixed race, usually claiming both black and Native American heritage, played key roles in the Union's success. One important turning point was the Battle of Honey Springs, fought on July 17, 1863, outside of present-day Muskogee. It was the first battle ever won by black soldiers and marked the first time regiments of whites, blacks, and Native Americans fought on the same field. The First Kansas Colored Volunteer Infantry Regiment joined white forces to win the day. Later, in his official report, General James G. Blunt would state that it was the black troops who were the deciding factor in the Union's victory. "Their coolness and bravery I have never seen surpassed [topped]," he later wrote.

An African-American family gathers in front of its makeshift cabin, marking a land claim near Guthrie in 1889.

After the Civil War, Congress created the all-black Ninth and Tenth Cavalries. Mostly veterans of the war, they were stationed at Forts Gibson and Sill. These troops, known as buffalo soldiers, performed many roles on the frontier. They helped build new forts, fought the many bandits hiding out in the territory, and chased down cattle thieves. They also patrolled Native American reservations and helped move Sooners off land they had illegally seized.

From 1865 to 1920, African Americans created more than fifty all-black towns, more than in all other states combined. Some of these towns were around for only a brief period. Others still exist today. For those escaping the shadow of slavery, Oklahoma was seen as a black paradise. African Americans could vote, study, and work with more ease and freedom than in most other states. Black Oklahomans were also encouraged to start businesses, which they did in great numbers. Before the Tulsa riot of 1921 temporarily destroyed the community, the mostly black section of town called Greenwood was also known as the Black Wall Street.

Oklahomans celebrate the many contributions African Americans have made to the state's vibrant and varied history.

Started by O.W. Gurley, Greenwood's 35 blocks were home to more than 11,000 residents, many of them prosperous business owners and millionaires.

In cities and towns, on the plains and the oil fields, black Oklahomans have made their lasting mark on the Sooner State. Today, Oklahoma's black community is as strong as ever. Many still come together to celebrate this legacy. Reunions, rodeos, and Juneteenth celebrations—which mark the freeing of many slaves—are just some of the ways Oklahomans celebrate their black pride.

Native Oklahoma

With more than 262,000 residents, it has the largest Native American population of any state. More than sixty nations are located within the state. Thirty-five of those nations have their official tribal councils in the state. But Oklahoma's Native residents are spread across the state. Most live in and around Tulsa and Oklahoma City. But many still live on reservations and in small communities throughout Oklahoma.

Many of the more than 252,000 Native Americans living in Oklahoma today are descendants of the original 67 groups inhabiting Indian Territory.

Despite their increased presence in the state, Oklahoma's Native residents still struggle to keep their culture and traditions alive. Recently members of the Absentee Shawnee Tribe met to create an economic plan covering the next five years. They also discussed how to develop their community and improve life for the tribe. "What it means is that we determine our own destiny, rather than being dependent upon the federal government," said tribal planner Eddie Brokeshoulder. Every year the Absentee Shawnee have received less and less federal funding. As the businesses owned by the tribe continue to thrive, the Absentee Shawnee have come to rely little on help from outside sources.

This is just one of many success stories the state's Native population has enjoyed. Still, tribal leaders keep an eye on the future. They urge Oklahoma's Native residents to take a more active role in the life and politics of the state. The first steps are registering to vote and being counted in the census, the totaling of all the people who live in the country. Without an accurate count of the Native American population, state officials may not realize the strength and power of the state's native communities. Tribal officials also argue that only by voting and helping to make and change laws can Oklahoma's Natives be sure their voices are heard.

Oklahomans Today

In the twenty-first century, the face of Oklahoma continues to change as the state welcomes newcomers from across the country and around the world. New times bring new concerns as the state's residents must adapt to a changing world economy. But like the brave settlers who endured the region's often harsh conditions, today's Oklahomans are working together to improve life in their state. They know that safe communities, strong schools, and thriving businesses are part of the formula for success. Together, Oklahomans are reaching their goals one step at a time.

As Oklahomans look to the future, they also honor the past and the rich cultural heritage that has helped to make them who they are.

Calendar of Events

Red Earth Native American Cultural Festival

Each May, Oklahoma City plays host to the largest Native American visual and performing arts event of its kind. It features art from more than 100 Native American nations as well as drum groups, dance competitions, and a parade with more than 1,500 Native dancers.

Chuck Wagon Gathering and Children's Cowboy Festival

At this Oklahoma City festival that kicks off in May, kids of all ages can try their hand at the cowpoke's life through activities such as learning how to make rope, designing bandanas, and weaving. Wagon rides and a Shetland pony carousel add to the fun as festival participants enjoy western entertainers and food from ten separate chuck wagons.

American Heritage Music Festival

Cloggers and fiddlers come to Grove each June to compete for cash prizes and the right to claim the title of grand champion. This weekend full of dancing and music is capped off by special performances each evening.

Aerospace America International Air Show

Each June, daring pilots take to the skies over Oklahoma City. Ranked as one of the world's top five air shows, this event features modern military jets, classic planes, and some of the best acrobatic pilots around. The highlight of the Friday-night show is a breathtaking blend of fireworks and flying.

A youth rodeo.

National Festival of the Puppeteers of America

This ancient art form is honored each year in June or July in Tahlequah. Puppeteers from around the world gather to celebrate their love of puppets. Performances, workshops, and exhibits are just some of the offerings at this weeklong event.

Woody Guthrie Folk Festival

This annual event kicks off each July in Okemah, the performer's hometown. It was started to promote Guthrie's music and to honor his legacy. Folk, alternative, and acoustic performers gather to take part in the tribute.

Balloon Fest

Hot-air balloons hover over Oklahoma City in August. But this festival is more than just balloons. With a rubber-duck race, food, crafts, kids' activities, music, exotic-animal displays, kite flying, skydiving demonstrations, free plane rides, bicycle stunt teams, and balloon races, this event offers something for everyone.

Arbuckle Mountain Bluegrass Festival

Head to Wynnewood for food, fun, and lots of bluegrass music. Festival goers are treated to some of the best bluegrass musicians performing today, plus some talented newcomers. But if you cannot make this September event, there is always the Spring Jam held in May and the Fall Jam in October.

Tulsa Oktoberfest

This fall festival has been going on for almost thirty years. It is truly an international affair with bands from Germany, Austria, and the United States. Highlights include a beer barrel race, a carnival, dancing, a parade, arts and crafts, and of course, a lot of great food.

A folk festival and craft show

4 How It Works

Oklahoma's constitution was adopted in 1907, when Oklahoma joined the Union. This important document contains a special measure called initiative and referendum. It means that the state's voters are allowed to suggest changes to the constitution. In addition, any changes to how the state is run must first be approved by the voters. This policy shows how seriously Oklahoma takes its citizens. Officials know it is important to hear the ideas and opinions of as many Oklahomans as possible. After all, new policies and laws affect the lives of all the state's citizens. The state government is committed to serving their needs.

How a Bill Becomes a Law

Oklahoma is a state that values the opinions of its citizens. Often they have their own ideas of changes that should be made or ways the state can be better run. The state's officials listen to the people who elected them. They also come up with their own ideas. But not everyone is always in agreement. Debate and compromise are important. And lawmakers have

This 17-foot bronze statue perched atop the state capitol in Oklahoma City is often called the Guardian. It honors the Native people who were the region's first residents.

Branches of Government

Executive The governor is the head of the state's executive branch. He or she is chosen by the state's voters to serve a four-year term. Voters also choose key officials who help the governor run the state. They include the lieutenant governor, attorney general, and the state treasurer.

Legislative Oklahoma's state legislature is made up of two parts. The senate has forty-eight members, each elected to a four-year term. The house of representatives is larger, with one hundred one members serving for two years each. Together the state's legislators make the laws all Oklahomans must follow.

Judicial The highest court in the state, the supreme court, has nine justices, or judges. They are appointed by the governor and then approved by the state's voters to their six-year terms. The state also has a court of appeals made up of at least twelve judges and a court of criminal appeals with five judges. They hear most of the state's legal cases.

the tough job of deciding what course the state should take in the future.

To make sure future laws are right for the state, the process by which a bill becomes a law involves many steps. That way, many voices and many opinions are considered. Bills are first proposed by a state senator or representative. He or she first presents the idea in written form. The bill is then discussed in the legislature. It is also often referred, or sent, to a special committee. Lawmakers serve on a variety of committees. They focus on specific topics the state must address, such as transportation, finance, or the environment. The committee members take the time to look into the bill more closely. They debate its strong points as well as its weaker parts. They suggest changes and ways the bill can be improved. During this stage in the process, the state's citizens are welcome to attend the meetings. They can make suggestions and offer their views on the possible law.

The state capitol has six floors and was built from 1914 to 1917. It is unique in that it is the only capitol that has working oil wells on its grounds.

After the committee is satisfied with the bill, it reports back to the legislature. The members of the legislature then have the chance to discuss the bill and make more changes. Finally the bill comes up for a vote. If it passes, the bill goes to the other part of the legislature. There, the bill goes through a similar process. It is examined, debated, and changed. Then it is voted on again. If the senators or representatives approve, the bill is one step closer to becoming a law.

Before it becomes an official state law, though, the governor must sign the bill. But he or she does not always agree with the legislature. If the governor is not in favor of the bill, he or she vetoes, or rejects, it. The bill then has one last chance to become a law. It returns to the legislature where two-thirds of each house must still be in favor of it. If the bill is passed, it then enters the law books. The bill is recorded, printed, and becomes an official part of Oklahoma law.

Local and County

Sooners serve their state in countless ways. The state is divided into seventy-seven counties. Each county is divided into districts. A commissioner, or government official, is elected from each of the districts. That way, the needs and concerns of the entire county are addressed. The commissioners work together to make sure county residents have access to services and programs. They also work to keep the people safe and to improve their lives. As one county's motto reads, "our mission is to provide friendly, professional services to citizens . . . of Oklahoma County." It is an important promise and one that Oklahoma's county officials take very seriously.

There are almost 600 cities and towns in the state. They require their own governing bodies, or groups, to make sure life runs smoothly. This usually takes the form of a city council. A group of the city's or town's residents is elected to oversee the day-to-day business of their community. Most of the state's cities also elect a mayor or a manager. He or she serves as the community leader, making sure the city spends it money wisely. The mayor must also prepare the city for the challenges of the future. He or she works to create jobs and find new sources of income for the community.

Even on the local level, Oklahomans are given a lot of control over their affairs. Cities with a population of more than 2,000 people can draw up and amend, or change, their own charters. A charter is a document listing how the community is to be run. Each city has its own unique set of needs and problems. By having the power to set their own laws and rules, the citizens of Oklahoma are able to tackle these concerns directly.

To find contact information for Oklahoma legislators go to this Web site: http://www5.lsb.state.ok.us/legislators/lsbaddress.asp If you are an Oklahoma resident you must enter your address information and click "Submit." The page then displays information about your state and federal legislators.

5 Making a Living

Oklahoma's economy is growing. Business leaders have turned to many sources of income and new businesses. The more varied the state's economy is, the healthier it will be now and in the future. New jobs require new skills and training, and Oklahomans are up to the task. They know their state is only as strong as the people working in it.

Agriculture

Although Oklahoma is known for its oil reserves, agriculture is just as important to the state. Almost three-quarters of Oklahoma's acreage is farmland. More than 70,000 farms and ranches dot the plains. Once, cotton was Oklahoma's chief crop. In recent years, wheat has taken its place as the state's most valuable farm product. Oklahoma currently ranks fourth nationwide in the production of winter wheat.

Oklahoma is a leading producer in many other categories as well. It ranks fifth in the production of pecans and eighth in the number of peaches it grows. Along the prairie plains, farms

Oklahoma City is one of the state's many business centers. The Myriad Botanical Gardens is just one of the many attractions that draw thousands of tourists each year to the capital.

in the Arkansas River valley produce spinach, beans, and carrots. In the Red River valley, cotton, peanuts, and a range of vegetables are the main crops. Corn and soybeans round out the list of the main foods raised in Oklahoma soil.

Despite the fact that the state is known for its oil reserves, agriculture is of major importance to Oklahoma. Irrigation helps to coax rows of growth from the often dry soil.

Recipe for a Peach Smoothie

Peaches are an important crop for many Oklahoma farmers. The following is a recipe that uses fresh peaches to make a tasty drink.

Ingredients:
2 medium-sized peaches, cut and pitted
1 banana, peeled
5 frozen strawberries
8 ounces of juice (either orange juice or
   pineapple juice)

Have an adult help you cut the peaches. Remove the pits from the peaches and place the fruit in a blender. Peel a ripe banana and place it in the blender. Take a package of frozen strawberries and drop five strawberries into the blender. Then pour 8 ounces of either orange or pineapple juice into the blender.

Have an adult help you use the blender to blend the ingredients. If the smoothie is too thick, you can add a little more juice. If the smoothie is too thin, you can add a scoop of vanilla ice cream to the blender, replace the top, and turn the blender on for another 20 seconds.

If you have other favorite fruits (such as blueberries, mangoes, papayas, or pineapples) you can substitute one of them for the strawberries and the banana. But some fruits (like apples or raisins) do not work very well in smoothies. Also some juices (such as apple juice) do not work as well as other juices. So ask an adult for advice if you want to add a different kind of fruit or juice to your smoothie. Then enjoy your refreshing drink!

The state's most valuable farm product is its cattle. More than 5 million heads of cattle graze the state's grasslands and fatten in the many feed lots. The state is the fourth-leading producer of cattle. Chickens, hogs, dairy cattle, and turkeys are also raised on the state's ranches and farms. In 2000, the state's agricultural products added $7.1 billion to the state's economy. That totals $1 billion more than in 1994. The key to the boost has been in adding value to farm and ranching products. In the past, the products were sent to businesses in other states to be processed or prepared. But over the past several years, many of the products have been processed in Oklahoma. This means that when the products are finally sold, the in-state businesses will receive more of the profits.

Mining

It comes as no surprise that Oklahoma is rich in mineral wealth. Oklahoma's economy was built on oil. In the 1920s, parts of the state led the nation in oil production. Though the petroleum industry has played less of a major role through the years, it is still a main employer statewide. Oil deposits are found in nearly every county in the state. But oil is not the only treasure stored in the earth. Natural gas is also found at most of the state's oil fields. In 1999, petroleum and natural gas production added $4.6 billion to the state's economy. The largest amounts of natural gas are found in the western part of the state. The state ranks third in natural gas production and fifth in oil. Pipelines are another source of employment. They help move the state's large supply of oil and gas. Workers are needed to build the lines and make sure they are secure to prevent any possible leaking.

Although oil reigns supreme in the Sooner State, Oklahoma has other valuable mineral resources as well. Rich beds of coal line parts of north-eastern and east-central Oklahoma.

There is a working oil well on the grounds of the state capitol in Oklahoma City. It is called Capitol Site Number 1.

Though Oklahoma is not a place well-known for its high altitudes, the state's various mountain chains provide valuable reserves of sand, gravel, limestone, gypsum, and salt. The sand and gravel are used for concrete and for highway building and repair. Limestone, often in the form of crushed stone, is also found in large quarries in the southwestern part of the state. Gypsum is used for construction and for products like fertilizer.

The strength of the state's economy is built on its large reserves of oil. Here, a new well is drilled near Guyman.

Products & Resources

Oil

Oklahoma was built on the strength of its oil reserves. The state's rich reserves helped fuel a growing international industry in petroleum and energy supply. In addition, new technology and new ways of pumping oil, now used worldwide, were first tested in Oklahoma.

Electronics

Electronic equipment ranks second among the state's manufactured products. Tulsa workers produce parts for motors as well as military communications systems. In Oklahoma City, telephone equipment is a major product, while television parts are made in factories in Shawnee.

Pecans

The state ranks fifth in the production of pecans. They grow mostly in groves on trees native to Oklahoma. The 1999 harvest produced a record-breaking 63 million pounds. The tasty nuts are sold to companies around the world.

Cattle

Beef cattle are the state's top agricultural earner. From raising the cows to processing the meat, cattle is the largest farm industry in the state, providing more than 105,000 jobs. More than 64,000 of the state's farms and ranches keep cattle, with the larger operations being found in the western part of the state.

Wheat

Oklahoma ranks fourth in the production of wheat. About 60 percent of the state's wheat is exported to countries around the world. The state's industry received an unexpected boost recently with the opening up of markets in China.

Peaches

Oklahoma's first shipments of peaches were headed out of the state within eight years of the territory's initial settlement. Today the state ranks eighth nationwide in the production of these fuzzy fruits.

69

Manufacturing

With so many natural resources in the state, Oklahoma's manufacturing industry thrives. It takes the state's various minerals and materials and increases their value by turning them into a wide range of products. Machinery is at the top of the list. Many factories across the state produce equipment used by the petroleum industry. Machine parts, construction equipment, and units used for heating and cooling are other top Oklahoma products as well.

Electronic items, such as telephone and television parts, rank second. Near many of the state's larger cities, factories churn out high-tech equipment including motor parts and communication systems used by the United States military. But

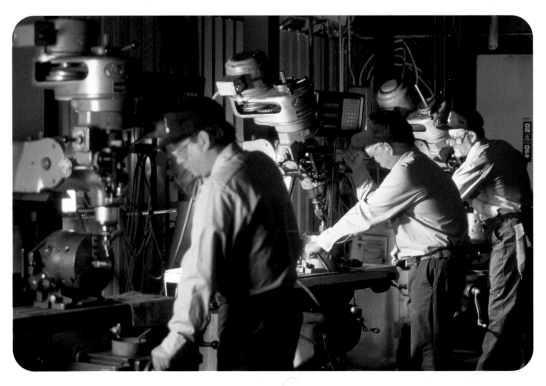

These operators are hard at work processing sheets of metal. The state's factories and manufacturing centers churn out a range of valuable products.

> Sooners are credited with inventing items that are now very important in everyday use. These inventions include the first shopping cart, the parking meter, the "Yield" sign, and the electric guitar.

the state produces a long list of manufactured items. Foods and metals are processed, rubber and plastic are turned into household items and tires, and transportation equipment is created. Factories near Tulsa and Oklahoma City also assemble cars and trucks and produce equipment for planes and spacecraft.

Tourism and Services

Tourism is a booming business in Oklahoma. People come from all over to visit the Sooner State and leave with a new sense of the variety and excitement the state has to offer. They bring their curiosity, enthusiasm, and their money. Tourism creates jobs and a wealth of businesses that help support countless families. Workers love sharing the best their state has to offer.

Newcomers to the state are presented with many options. Do you explore the canyons and ranches of northwestern Oklahoma or take in the mountains, forests, and scenic waterfalls that mark the southern portion of the state? For those who are drawn to city life, Tulsa is an excellent choice.

Curious tourists have many places to explore in the Oklahoma, such as the Great Salt Plains in the northern part of the state. Visitors can dig for crystals and rocks hidden among the salt flats.

It is a busy city that manages to hold on to its casual, laid-back appeal. It is also home to two unique and lesser known museums. The Gilcrease Museum preserves Native American art and artifacts, while the Philbrook Museum has more than 8,500 works in its collection. The Philbrook is housed in a restored 1920s villa on 23 peaceful acres in the heart of the city.

This zookeeper, one of Oklahoma's many service workers, earns money for the state while offering the public a glimpse at creatures not normally found in the region.

Services are a key part of Oklahoma's economy. In fact, they account for the largest portion of the state's income. People who work in this industry are providing a service to customers and the public. Most service jobs are found in or near the state's major urban areas. But across Oklahoma people work in a variety of service roles. They are employed in department stores and supermarkets. They sell food, grain, or oil products. They provide fellow Oklahomans with cars, insurance, and new homes. These are just a few of the many ways the state's workers earn their living.

Service workers help make people's lives easier. Some supply the products and utilities that Oklahomans use every day. There would be no water, electricity, gas, or phone lines in the state's homes if it were not for service employees. But they make up just a fraction of the state's service jobs. Pilots and flight attendants, teachers, nurses, hair stylists, mechanics—the list of jobs Oklahomans fill is endless.

The state's land, its valuable resources and its rich history are all a gift to the people of Oklahoma. They have learned from the struggles and triumphs of the past and—filled with Sooner strength and determination—turn a bright face to the future.

Future generations will inherit an Oklahoma built strong by the hard work and determination of the state's many dedicated residents.

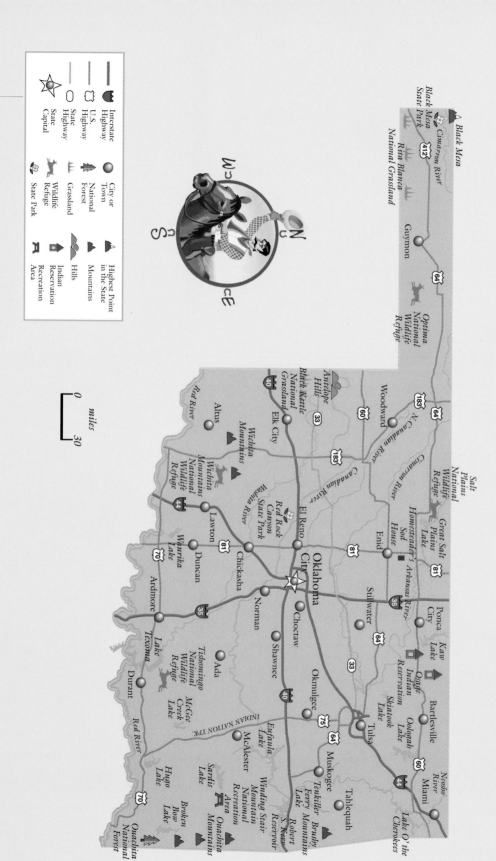

OKLAHOMA

Legend

Interstate Highway
U.S. Highway
State Highway
State Capital

City or Town
National Forest
Wildlife Refuge
State Park

Highest Point in the State
Mountains
Grassland
Indian Reservation

Mountains
Hills
Wildlife Refuge
Recreation Area

N
NW
NE
W
E
SW
SE
S

0 miles 30

Black Mesa
Black Mesa State Park
Cimarron River
112
Rita Blanca National Grassland
Guymon
64
Optima National Wildlife Refuge

Red River
Altus
Antelope Hills
40
Black Kettle National Grassland
Elk City
33
Woodward
183
60
Salt Plains National Wildlife Refuge
64
N. Canadian River
Cimarron River
Great Salt Plains Lake
Salt Plains National Wildlife Refuge
Wichita Mountains
183
Washita River
Canadian River
Homesteader's Sod House
Arkansas River
Wichita Mountains National Wildlife Refuge
44
Red Rock Canyon State Park
El Reno
Enid
81
81
Lawton
81
Chickasha
Oklahoma City
35
Stillwater
64
Ponca City
Kaw Lake
70
Duncan
Waurika Lake
Norman
Choctaw
33
Osage Indian Reservation
Skiatook Lake
Oologah Lake
Bartlesville
Ardmore
35
Shawnee
Okmulgee
75
Tulsa
64
60
Miami
Neosho River
41
Lake Texoma
Ada
McGee Creek Lake
Tishomingo National Wildlife Refuge
Eufaula Lake
McAlester
Muskogee
Tenkiller Ferry Lake
Robert S. Kerr Reservoir
Brushy Lake
Tahlequah
Lake O' the Cherokees
Durant
Red River
INDIAN NATION TPK.
Sardis Lake
Winding Stair Mountains National Recreation Area
70
Broken Bow Lake
Ouachita Mountains
Ouachita National Forest

74

An Osage shield stands in the center of the blue background on the state's flag. The shield is covered with two symbols of peace. A traditional Native American peace pipe is crossed by an olive branch. The word Oklahoma appears below the many feathers hanging from the shield. The flag was officially adopted in 1925.

A white star appears in the center of the state seal. In its center, a settler and an Native American shake hands. They stand for the spirit of peace and cooperation that exists among all the peoples of Oklahoma. On the star's five points are symbols of each of the Five Civilized Tribes brought to the state in the early 1800s. Around the star are forty-five smaller, yellow stars. They stand for each of the states that entered the Union before Oklahoma became the forty-sixth state. The seal was adopted in 1907.

State Flag and Seal

Oklahoma

Words by Oscar Hammerstein II
Music by Richard Rodgers

Brand new State! Brand new State!

gon - na treat you great! _____ Gon - na give you

bar - ley, Car - rots and per - ta - ters, Pas - ture fer the cat - tle,

Spin - ach and ter - may - ters! Flow - ers on the prair - ie where the June bugs

zoom, Plen' - y of air and plen' - y of room,

Plen' - y of room to swing a rope! _____ Plen' - y of

heart and plen' - y of hope. _____

CHORUS

O _____ k - la - hom - a, where the

More About Oklahoma

Books

Antle, Nancy. *Beautiful Land: A Story of the Oklahoma Land Rush.* New York: Viking, 1994.

Giordano, Geraldine. *The Oklahoma City Bombing.* New York: Rosen, 2003.

Isaacs, Sally Senzell. *The Great Land Rush.* Chicago: Heinemann, 2003.

Thompson, Kathleen. *Oklahoma.* Austin, TX: Raintree Steck-Vaughn, 1996.

Web Sites

Official Oklahoma Tourism Site
http://www.travelok.com

Oklahoma's Official Web Site
http://www.ok.gov

Oklahoma Scenic Rivers—Kids' Corner
http://www.scenicrivers.state.ok.us/kids.asp

About the Author

Doug Sanders is a writer and editor who lives in New York City. His favorite places to visit in the Sooner State are the Wichita Mountains and the memorial to the victims of the Oklahoma City bombing.

Index

Page numbers in **boldface** are illustrations.